QUESTIONS THAT REFUSE TO GO AWAY

PEACE·AND·JUSTICE·SERIES 13

QUESTIONS THAT REFUSE TO GO AWAY

Peace and Justice in North America

MARIAN C. FRANZ

HERALD PRESS
Scottdale, Pennsylvania
Waterloo, Ontario

Library of Congress Cataloging-in-Publication Data
Franz, Marian Claassen, 1930-
    Questions that refuse to go away / Marian Claassen Franz.
       p.   cm. — (Peace and justice series ; 13)
    Includes bibliographical references.
    ISBN 0-8361-3558-X
    1. Peace—Religious aspects—Christianity. 2. Christianity and
justice. 3. Church and social problems. I. Title. II. Series.
BT736.4.F685   1991
261.8'73'0973—dc20   91-10197
                                                            CIP

The paper used in this publication is recycled and meets the minimum requirements of American National Standard for Information Sciences—Permanence of Paper for Printed Library Materials, ANSI Z39.48-1984.

Unless otherwised marked, Scripture quotations are from the *Holy Bible: New International Version.* Copyright © 1973, 1978, 1984 International Bible Society. Used by permission of Zondervan Bible Publishers.

Excerpt marked RSV is from the Revised Standard Version of the Bible, copyright 1946, 1952, 1971 by the Division of Christian Education of the National Council of the Churches of Christ in the USA. Used by permission.

QUESTIONS THAT REFUSE TO GO AWAY
Copyright © 1991 by Herald Press, Scottdale, Pa. 15683
    Published simultaneously in Canada by Herald Press,
    Waterloo, Ont. N2L 6H7. All rights reserved.
Library of Congress Catalog Number: 91-10197
International Standard Book Number: 0-8361-3558-X
Printed in the United States of America
Cover and book design by Gwen M. Stamm

1 2 3 4 5 6 7 8 9 10 96 95 94 93 92 91

To Gregory, Gayle, and Coretta.
Very special persons.

Contents

Foreword

The church of North America consists of congregations in Canada and the United States. These congregations are called to be divine leaven in the dough of human experience.

We see how easily governments spend billions on wars to maintain influence, protect affluent lifestyles, and endure access to such vital natural resources as oil. We see how quickly nations turn toward military action to crush perceived enemies.

We also observe how reluctant governments are to work at peacemaking and negotiating which yield creative resolutions of conflict. We note how slow governments are to spend money and energy on social problems even as the numbers of homeless people enters the millions, poverty leaves stomachs empty and spirits shriveled, and despair yields soaring murder rates.

How are congregations to be leaven in this tough dough? How do they call governments away from the missiles, warplanes, and tanks?

How do they call back toward justice societies

which seem to have lost their capacity for moral outrage?

How do they help a nation unite as quickly behind the healing of wounds as behind the waging of war?

When the laws of the nation promote violence and not peace, a numbed and calloused people rather than a just people, is there a time to disobey human law and thus obey God's law?

This book explores such complex questions in simple and accessible ways. Although its focus is on North America, we trust its insights will be useful in the many nations whose governments and congregations must deal with issues it addresses.

> —*Michael A. King*
> *Philadelphia, Pennsylvania*

CHAPTER 1

How Can We Strengthen the Rainbow Covenant?

This book is about questions, ancient questions. The same questions have faced each generation attempting to keep covenant with God.

These questions refuse to go away. If we push them aside, they stubbornly return. Although the questions may be old, the situations are new for each generation. We cannot avoid the choices the questions present. Not to choose is to choose.

When we ask the old questions in new situations, we find surprises. Who is Noah? What is our flood? What is the ark? What is the rainbow?

Who Was Noah?

The rainbow covenant began with Noah (Gen. 6:9-9:29). Noah was probably not an expert on rain, animals, or ship building. Noah was a person who listened to and followed the call of God to *save all species*. Now that all the species are again threatened, perhaps Noah's situation can help us with our questions.

What Is Our Flood?

According to the Bible, life on the earth was destroyed because "the earth was corrupt . . . and *was full of violence*" (emphasis added). This violence threatened all creation, so judgment came through a flood of water (Gen. 7, 8, emphasis added).

If you flood the earth with violence, the earth will flood you. The haunting words of the Negro spiritual come to mind. "God gave the earth a rainbow sign, no more water, the fire next time." In the first flood, only God had the right and power to destroy the earth.

Although even today only God has that right, we now have the power to destroy the earth with a flood of fire. Like Noah, our call is to save all species from this flood of nuclear violence.

What Is the Ark?

The ark we are talking about is not the one that landed atop Mt. Ararat. Our ark is the planet itself, an extraordinary work of art. The health of this delicate balance of air, water, and minerals supporting all plant and animal life is in our hands. It is our physical ark.

Like the first ark, the future of this second ark depends on whether its inhabitants can live in peace. The end of the Cold War gives hope that they may. Yet new wars threaten. If the ark's inhabitants cannot live in peace, the flood of fire is near.

Suppose the elephant, to show power, had stamped her foot on the floor of Noah's ark. Suppose the lions had eaten the lambs. Or suppose woodpeckers had not been persuaded to look at interests other than their own. It is hard to get along on arks. It gets harder as they become more crowded.

"We wouldn't be able to stand the smell of the ark," one writer said, "if it weren't for the flood outside." We might give up the hard work of being peacemakers on the ark today if it weren't for the threat of a flood of fire.

What Is the Rainbow?

Those who have seen a nuclear explosion say it has terrifying beauty. Electromagnetic impulses cause flashes of light above the mushroom cloud. They appear in *all the colors of the rainbow.* "It is," said one observer, "the rainbow shattered into a million bits.

Is it possible to shatter the rainbow? "Indeed not!" I want to shout. The rainbow is a symbol of the covenant: "I will be your God. I call you to be my people. While the earth lasts, cold and heat . . . summer and winter . . . shall not cease!"

Yet the findings of nuclear scientists make earlier predictions about the flood, terrible as they were, seem optimistic. The firing of nuclear missiles by just one country could trigger nuclear winter. Debris and smoke from the explosions high in the atmosphere would cloud the earth from the sun's rays. There would be no springtime of growing crops, no summertime of harvest. All life would be endangered.

As a child, I used to ponder the rainbow with fellow

eight-year-old philosophers. The rainbow was really a complete circle, I thought, with only half of it visible. I now know I was right. From an airplane I have seen the rainbow from above. It is indeed a complete circle!

"I am your God. I call you to be my people," the covenant states. We hold up the other half of the rainbow by keeping God's covenant. But this half of the rainbow is in trouble. How can we reinforce our half?

I have seen a complete circular rainbow in another place. Members of the Hiroshima peace movement in Japan use the circular rainbow as their symbol. The whole circular rainbow is indeed our symbol of hope.

The dangers of a nuclear flood are known—yet are not accepted because of something called *denial*. Denial is acting as if something that exists doesn't exist.

"As in the Days of Noah"

Jesus noted that in the days of Noah, "the people were eating, drinking, marrying, and going about business as usual" (Matt. 24:37-38). They knew nothing about the flood until it happened. They were caught off-guard. They looked the other way, ignoring the corruption that filled the earth with violence.

We must help others to see the danger of nuclear flood. We must confront the elephants and lions and woodpeckers on our ark who undermine its safety. We must point to a covenant which alone can save us from a flood of destruction. We will help to keep the rainbow promise—an earth on which summertime and winter, seedtime and harvest do not cease.

CHAPTER 2

Which King Will You Serve?

"We have no king but Caesar!" the enemies of Jesus cried. Their cry announced a decision.

"Shall I crucify your king?" a puzzled Pilate wanted to know. "Which side are you on?"

No one in the crowd could delay choice. Is Jesus or Caesar your emperor?

Their choice? "We have no king but Caesar!"

Some people of Barmen, Germany, took the opposite position. They chose a king who was not Caesar. They chose the principles of Jesus Christ over Hitler's laws. Their story becomes more relevant each day.

During the dark days of Hitler's power, a courageous group of Christians met in Germany in 1934. The Barmen Declaration takes its name from Barmen, the town in which it was written. Those who wrote it were persecuted by Hitler because of their action. This remarkable gathering of Christians called themselves by an appropriate name: "The Confessing Church."

The authors of the Barmen Declaration took their name from the "confessions" of early Christians who suffered persecution. The complaint against the early Christians, you will remember, was that they "turned the world upside down."

Actually they were turning it right-side-up, but people whose values are upside down do not want to be disturbed. They will tell you to keep your faith to yourself. If you insist on putting your faith into action, they will resist it, sometimes with brutal force. The Jesus-or-Caesar decision was, for the early Christians, often a life-or-death choice.

This time of decision, great danger, and severe testing was called a *status confessionis*, or "time appropriate for confession." This confession showed why a person had chosen to resist the government. It clarified the faith which led the person to costly decision. With the loving support of the Christian community, the person also wrote about corporate faith in the body of Christ (see 1 Tim. 6:12-13 and Heb. 4:14; 10:23).

By the time the Confessing Church met in Barmen, Hitler had gained firm control and a faithful following. Most of Germany supported him—the business community, the universities, the churches.

Yes, even the churches. Many had rallied around Hitler's call to "fight godless communism." The national suspicion, fear, and hatred turned in on itself. It also included anything Jewish, antiwhite, or anti-German. To pursue Hitler's "just cause," any atrocity was allowed. Millions died brutal deaths.

A group calling itself "German Christians" gave the Nazi regime their blessing. They received high positions in the Nazi government. They, along with the Nazi party, attempted to make the whole German church an arm of the government. All German churches were to have one church government, with no regard to individual differences. The new church government would be patterned after the Nazi party.

But these "German Christians" did not represent all Christians of Germany. The Confessing Church at Barmen represented all groups within the German Evangelical Church who opposed Hitler and the "German Christians."

At Barmen there were 139 delegates from the Lutheran, Reformed, and United Churches. They asked, is this our *status confessionis*? Is it time to declare that our faith in Christ prevents our following the government?

Agreeing it was, they issued a formal protest based on the Bible. Like the confessions of early Christians, theirs would let people know why the Confessing Church must stand against its government. Like the early Christians, they suffered persecution.

All Pharaohs with upside-down values give the same response. "Keep your faith in God as a mental exercise. Go along. Don't meddle." The courageous statement of the Confessing Church was too late to stop the growth and power of the Nazi movement.

Others continued to resist and also suffered persecution. (Karl Barth, Dietrich Bonhoeffer, Martin Niemoller, Father Alfred Delp, S.J., Frantz Jaegerstatter, Raul Lichtenberg, to name a few.) One spent sev-

en years at Dachau, the infamous Nazi concentration
camp. Others died in Nazi prisons or as draftees.

Since we know that Hitler considered the signers of
the Barmen Confession worthy of persecution and
death, we are curious to read it. What horrible things
did the Confessing Church say that made him per-
secute or kill them? Here is a sample.

> Jesus Christ, as he is attested for us in Holy Scripture, is
> the one Word of God which we have to hear and
> which we have to trust and obey in life and in
> death. . . .
>
> We reject the false doctrine, as though the Church
> could and would have to acknowledge as a source of its
> proclamation, apart from and beside the one Word of
> God, still other events and powers, figures, and truths,
> as God's revelation. . . .
>
> Jesus Christ is God's mighty claim upon our whole life.
> Through him we receive the joyful deliverance from
> the godless fetters of this world for a free, grateful ser-
> vice to his creatures. . . .
>
> As the church of pardoned sinners it has to testify in
> the midst of a sinful world, with its faith and with its
> obedience, with its message and with its order, that it is
> solely his property."[1]

The shocking thing about the Barmen Declaration
is that it isn't shocking! Its tone is not angry at all. It
does not even mention Hitler. How could these soft
words provoke such a cruel, harsh response?

This is why: the Confession says yes to God, no to
false gods. To say yes to Jesus Christ was to say no to

Hitler and all he represented. Hitler understood that when they said "Christ is our Fuehrer" (Lord) they also implied that "Hitler is not our Fuehrer."

What was the Barmen Declaration's tremendous power? Look again at the verbs in the first paragraph: hear, trust, and obey. The Confessing Church was straining to hear the voice of God and calling on fellow Christians to listen also.

A deeper listening was required in this crisis situation. Hearing must move to trust. When we trust, we rely so completely on what we hear that we are willing to risk our life on it. It is better to surrender one's life than to surrender trust.

Hearing and trusting are the roots for a flowering obedience. They call for real action in the real world. Loving God is both a physical and a mental exercise. An inward journey of faith results in an outward journey of obedience and action. When we obey we follow through on what we hear and trust. No matter what.

The path of trust and obedience is like mountain climbing. The mountain climber firmly places one foot before searching for higher ground with the other. When the foot of faith is firmly placed, the foot of action searches at some risk for unfamiliar new footing. When it finds it, the foot of faith again searches for and moves to a new level.

Similarly, biblical study must be followed by more faithful action in the real world. Now new risks drive one to more study and call for new discernment. This then leads to more faithful action. And so on and on.

The more faithful our obedience, the deeper our trust. The deeper the trust, the more we are willing to risk for the sake of making peace, for the sake of those on the edge of society. Risk becomes a natural part of the Christian vocabulary and lifestyle.

How Does the Barmen Declaration Help Us to Ask the Old Questions in a New Way?

At times the church finds itself in a *status confessionis*, a confessional situation in which it must take sides, clearly and firmly. It must answer the question, "Is Jesus or Caesar your emperor?" and explain its choice. The Barmen Declaration set an example.

Barmen proved that churches with differing theological positions can present a common confession. As the spokes of a wheel get closer near the hub, so in a dangerous and idolatrous situation God brings believers together.

The clear "no" of the Barmen Declaration was also a "yes." My favorite part is, "Jesus Christ is God's mighty claim upon our whole life. Through him we receive the joyful deliverance from the godless fetters of this world for a free, grateful service to his creatures."

The phrase, "we reject the false doctrine," is repeated six times in the Barmen Declaration. The "German Christians" who cast their lot with the Nazi party had seized authority in the church. The Confessing Church exposed the heresies and injustices. The Confessing Church testified to the truth of God and stated that the church must be free to stand on the words of its own confessions.

The Barmen Declaration went beyond any previous church statement to stress the independence of the church from state control. "The church is solely God's property," it declared.

To obey God, the Confessing Church had to disobey the state. Those who obeyed the state did not serve God. Neither did they serve their state. They only helped the state destroy itself.

The Confessing Church faced two dangers. One was persecution from the outside. The other was even more deadly: silence on the inside—to slip into trust in the false gods of the time. Members of the Confessing Church well knew that the costs of their confession could be high. But they could not be silent when the false god of the state tried to replace God. They would hear, trust, and obey in "life and in death."

How is the Barmen Declaration relevant to us? Barmen is just one example of Christian public opposition to government. Many Christians all over the world are taking heroic, costly, and redemptive stands to define their faith and the limits of state authority.

We are tempted to ask why the Confessing Church waited until it was too late to stop the Nazi regime. Or we might ask how such blindness by the "German Christians" was possible.

However, the question returns like a boomerang, for there is a dark similarity between the Third Reich and our own situation. The blind confidence in military strength is the same. Have we North Americans spoken in time about a nuclear holocaust that can burn, not packed furnaces, but packed cities?

Might it be time for a new Barmen Declaration? Is this our time for confession? There are times when, like the early Christians and those who framed the Barmen Confession, we too must say "no." Why? Because we have already said yes to the voice of God whom we hear, trust, and obey "in life and death."

A new confessing church will not seek martyrdom. But it will be prepared to go to prison and death rather than support the state in crimes against humanity and God's planet.

Questions That Refuse to Go Away:

1. List reasons this may be a time for a new confessing church.

2. List possible actions when national political interests and commitment to biblical faith conflict.

3. When should the church:

   a. Confess that in some areas the state's policies are better than its own?

   b. Confront the state with its clear understanding of the will of God?

   c. Resist the state because it tries to take God's place in our lives?

   d. Confront fellow Christians who have become instruments of unjust government policy?

   e. Disobey the state to obey God?

4. Might persecution be an appropriate price to pay as one chooses to turn away from false gods that threaten to end all life on earth?

5. Like the Barmen confessors before us, how might we speak out clearly and suffer to protest false trust in deadly weapons?

6. Bonhoeffer (who was killed for his resistance) said the church should give three responses to unjust actions of the state: Call on the state to be just. Help the victims of injustice. Try to stop injustice. How does the church do this today?

CHAPTER 3

Lord, Is It I?

Everything was ready. The atomic bomb was on the plane. The flight crew had just been told that the target would be Hiroshima. Only one thing remained. The crew bowed their heads and heard the chaplain's prayer. "May the men who fly this night be kept safe in your care, and may they be returned safely to us."

But who prayed for the people in Hiroshima? Bizarre deaths awaited tens of thousands of them. And who prayed for the thousands more who would suffer the unspeakable agony of lifelong injuries and lifelong grief?

Who prayed for those whose eyes would melt because of a light brighter than a thousand suns?

Who prayed for the nuns on the way to the cathedral for their daily prayers?

Who prayed for the beautiful children whose loving parents were placing school lunches in their hands and kisses on their cheeks?

The flight crew did return safely. The chaplain has since repented of his participation. But have the nations?

All the bombs dropped on all the cities of World War II equalled two million tons of TNT—two megatons. For six years the destruction rained from the skies.[2] Today there are 10,000 megatons in the arsenals of the world. It would take not six years, but one hour to bring the flood of ruin. A World War II every second. No place on the planet is safe.

We cannot wrap our minds around the enormous suffering of the thousands in Hiroshima. Yet the total fire power in today's world arsenals is equal to a million Hiroshimas! Governments continue to build them even though there are only 3,000 cities of that size. There is already enough destructive power to kill a hundred billion people. But there are only about five billion people on the planet.

The weapons exceed the targets! During the six months it took the U.S. to ratify the INF disarmament treaty, the U.S. and the Soviet Union deployed more nuclear weapons than will be eliminated under the treaty—less than 5 percent of their combined nuclear arsenals. The only thing the treaty did was put a tiny dent in the stockpile we had just created. Meanwhile, we kept producing as many weapons as we had for years—three to five nuclear weapons every day, each more accurate, more deadly, more costly.[3]

What have we done? Where have we been? Are the holes in our moral sieves so large that they do not strain out boulders? Do they allow sins the size of Hiroshimas to pass through them?

Jesus referred to such sieves. People in his day put their drinking water through sieves to strain out gnats. Jesus accused them of straining out the gnats but swallowing camels. Was he talking about us? Can we say that the nuclear death threat came so gradually that we did not notice? Are the holes in our moral sieves elastic? Have they gradually stretched open enough to let the whole world fall through?

Who Is Responsible?

Modern weapons vastly increase the awful "efficiency" of murder. They also further distance the killers from the results of their deeds. Bomber squadrons can destroy block after block of whole cities, then their pilots can return to their officers' clubs to celebrate. Now people have trained to kill billions on other continents with the turn of a key. Is this not demonic?

To design this destruction, hundreds of thousands of engineers work at drawing boards. Scientists and engineers look for that final breakthrough in technology. They design weapons and calculate thousands of deaths at computer terminals in air-conditioned offices.

The war economy provides comfortable jobs for millions of employees in and out of military uniform. Contractors make easy profits. The jobs of millions of factory workers depend on this military terrorism. Employees go to work in the morning and routinely manufacture these murderous weapons. They return home at night with paychecks that feed and educate their families.

That is how, one by one, these horrible weapons are

produced. That is how, steadily and increasingly, warfare and murder enter the daily fabric of modern North American life.

The question of this chapter is not "Who is to blame?" but "Who is responsible?" Only those without sin are allowed to cast stones. If we pick up a stone of blame we will miss the opportunity to learn important lessons about ourselves. The challenge for us is to stop assessing blame and start assuming responsibility.

When the disciples learned that their Lord was to be betrayed, they did not blame. Each asked the question that would not go away: "Lord, is it I?"

It is tempting to suppose that distance absolves us from responsibility. The confessors at Barmen did not say, "It's not our fault. We are not Nazis, and furthermore, we always abhorred their policies." Instead of washing their hands, they accepted responsibility and spoke the costly truth.

Chaplain Zabelka, who prayed for the crew that dropped the bomb on Hiroshima, asked the questions that refused to go away. He declared his own confession. Here are parts of it.

> I, like the Catholic pilot of the Nagasaki plane . . . was heir to a Christianity that had for seventeen hundred years engaged in revenge, murder, torture, the pursuit of power, the prerogative of violence, all in the name of our Lord. The mainline Christian churches still teach something that Christ never taught or even hinted at, namely the just war theory, a theory that to me has been completely discredited theologically, historically, and psychologically.
>
> It never entered my mind to publicly protest the

consequences of these massive air raids. I was told it was necessary; told openly by the military and told implicitly by my church's leadership. To the best of my knowledge, no American cardinals or bishops were opposing these mass air raids. Silence in such matters, especially by the public body like the American bishops, is a stamp of approval. . . . Why, after I finished chaplaincy school at Harvard, I had my military chalice officially blessed by the then Bishop Cushing of Boston. How much more clearly could the message be given?

To fail to speak to the utter moral corruption of the mass destruction of civilians was to fail as a Christian and as a priest as I see it. Hiroshima and Nagasaki happened in and to a world and a Christian church that had asked for it—that had prepared the moral consciousness of humanity to do and to justify the unthinkable. . . . The operational moral atmosphere in the church in relation to mass bombing of enemy civilians was totally indifferent, silent, and corrupt at best—at worst it was religiously supportive of these activities by blessing those who did them.

Chaplain Zabelka believes,

Communion with Christ cannot be established on disobedience to his clearest teachings. Jesus authorized none of his followers to substitute violence for love. . . .

The church should clearly declare:

that war is totally incompatible with Jesus' teaching and that Christians cannot and will not engage in or pay for it from this point in history on. This would have the effect of putting all nations on this planet on notice that from now on they are going to have to conduct their mutual slaughter without Christian support—physical, financial, or spiritual.[4]

Questions That Will Not Go Away:

1. What motivates destruction of human life?

2. Who bears the responsibility before God? Only those who pull the trigger? Those who press the buttons? Those who set policy? Those who give orders? Those who transmit the orders? Those who obey orders? Those who manufacture the weapons? Those who pay the taxes? Those who say little or nothing?

3. How can we restore a human face to a world gone mad with violence carried out by technology?

4. Individuals usually deny personal responsibility for the actions of large organizations. How can we encourage individuals to help change bad organizational policies?

5. Since governments spend so much time and money on weapons of death, how might the churches make a Barmen-type declaration?

CHAPTER 4

Are We Turning Plowshares into Swords?

Much North American violence has its roots in unequal distribution of wealth. And our national economy is closely tied to military expenses.

Perhaps an image of a train can help us to understand the connection between economic and military violence.

Imagine all the people of the world as passengers on an immense train. On this train, a few passengers, mainly in the advanced countries, ride in the first-class coaches. The other passengers, however, are crammed into cattle cars at the rear. They cannot imagine the comfort in the first-class cars.

The conditions in the cattle cars rapidly grow worse. Whether the first-class passengers have stopped to think about it or not, the deprived millions have paid for the first-class comforts with their misery and poverty.

About 15 million children die each year for lack of food and inexpensive vaccines—over 40,000 children a day, 28 each minute. More have died from starvation in the last five years than in the last 150 years before that.[5]

Albert Camus, a Frenchman, wrote about the military violence of modern weapons. He said that leaders of the world, the engineers of the train, are peacefully seated in a train speeding toward an abyss at a thousand miles an hour. Because of the poverty in the rear of the train, the train is careening toward doom.

The link between economic and military violence is clear. The nations that grow strong through weapons do so at the expense of the poor. More and more we see that this slow economic death is silent murder.

A cartoon pictures a grandly attired king on his throne being addressed by a servant.

Messenger: "In reviewing the budget, O King, I find you have allocated billions for defense and not one cent for the poor."

"Right!" thunders the king. "When the rebellion comes, I'll be ready."

The folly of the king's choice is obvious. By directing resources from human needs to armaments, the king only hastens rebellion. His military expenditure is causing the very thing it is supposed to avoid.

That simple lesson is not always obvious to us.

Who really pays the price for enormous military appetites? Former U.S. President Eisenhower, who was World War II's top military general, knew.

Every gun that is made, every warship launched, every

rocket fired signifies, in the final sense, a theft from those who hunger and are not fed, those who are cold and not clothed.

The size of that theft is shown by world military expenditures.

If I gave you $1 million, told you to spend it at the rate of $1,000 a day, and told you to come back when it was gone, you would not be back for nearly three years. If you spent $1 billion at that rate you would not be back for nearly 300 years.

In the early 1990s, even before the war in the Persian Gulf, the U.S. spent *in one year alone* $304 billion for current military expenditures and another $184 billion for past military (debts on past wars, veterans benefits, etc.). At $1,000 a day it would take you 1336 *centuries* to spend the total.[6]

What the world spends in just ten days on military hardware would feed all the world's hungry for a whole year.

Not only that. There would be enough left over to provide each hungry person with clean water.

Not only that. They could also be provided with good health care.

Not only that. Each could have adequate housing and, on top of that, an education.[7]

That is the enormity of our sin!

Swords are to be turned into plowshares that produce food, not the reverse. The biblical vision has been turned inside out. As the military coffers grow fatter, the diet of the poor grows leaner. While military expenditures grow, so do the numbers of those who are hungry, sick, and homeless.

Swords Instead of Bread

While these weapons kill without a trigger being pulled, the current energy supply is also being depleted. We are failing to develop new resources of energy. We fail to give attention to the needs of people so they can become productive persons. And these problems grow worse as military spending increases.

We waste resources—money, energy, brains—that should be applied to more urgent problems. Racial injustices and separation are becoming more pronounced and foster an escalation of white racism. Some decaying urban communities inhabited by poor minorities look as if bombs have already fallen. Minority unemployment continues to increase.

Sadly, like the foolish king, we prepare for war to make ourselves secure and end up insecure.

As Christians see the connection between fat military budgets and lean children, they ask questions.

These Questions Will Not Go Away:

1. What groups in society suffer most because of "defense" spending?

2. What have we Christians from richer nations and classes to say to those in the poorer nations and classes who pay the price of our luxury?

3. Might we be so greedy as to destroy ourselves rather than share our wealth?

4. Have the military costs become so high that they undermine the very values they are to defend?

5. Who is the Lazarus at your gate? (Luke 16:19-31)

6. "Lord, when did we see you . . ." exploited? (Matt. 25:31-46).

CHAPTER 5

Can We Replace the Nightmare with a Vision?

A global nightmare is created when we base our security on violence, or the threat of it. Against that nightmare stands the biblical vision. Have we Christians not a dream with the power of life to take us beyond conventional wisdom? It is hard to see visions while living in a nightmare, but that gift was given at Pentecost. "The young shall see visions and the old shall dream dreams." The vision is based on truth.

The suffering of our time is so immense it can overwhelm us. Imagine the economic violence of 40,000 children dying every day from malnutrition. Imagine the grief of parents who can only watch them die. Grasp the military violence of the death of whole continents.

It is easier not to think about it, to feel nothing. To feel nothing is to be hard-hearted, to have a deadened conscience. Because the pain is so depressing, it can lead to despair.

Silly Optimism—Costly Hope

Despair, however, has a useful purpose. Embrace it to move beyond it. It is the only way to lose the numbness and soften the hardened conscience. It is the only way to move to hope.

Despair allows us to cry to God "out of the depths." Despair allows us to grieve with God over the brokenness of the rainbow. Despair awakens the conscience. Despair moves us from silly optimism to costly hope.

A silly optimism glibly says of nuclear "flood," "Don't worry. Be happy. God won't let it happen."

A silly optimism uses faith as a happiness pill. God is a giant aspirin. "Take God twice a day and you won't feel any pain."

A silly optimism says, "There will always be wars and rumors of wars." It forgets the call to be peace manufacturers.

A silly optimism says of hunger, "The poor you will always have with you." It lacks the will to even contemplate a vision.

Some Christians *expect* injustice, violence, and destruction of nature to increase. They expect the nuclear flood and believe its coming at our own hand is taught by the Bible. According to this end-time thinking, the prospect of all-out nuclear war and final nuclear winter heralds the second coming of Christ.

These persons think that, as true believers, they are exempt and safe from the suffering or "tribulation" that will befall others. They have little concern to be peacemakers, to care for the globe's threatened species, to try to stay the flood.

They act as though Christ did not tell us the "times

and seasons" are not for us to know. As though God's kingdom is not worked out in history as well as beyond it. Silly optimism produces no vision.

A costly hope comes from hearing, trusting, obeying. The secret of our costly hope rests on a powerful vision which transcends, a dream which has the power of life. "Behold, I do a new thing. Can you not perceive it?" (Isa. 43:19). The call of this vision is to turn the winter of violence into the springtime of planting.

The Nightmare Ends Where Compassion Begins

"As you did it unto one of the least of these. . . ." That is the beginning of vision. We then ask, "Who is the Lazarus at my gate?" We begin to connect the statistics with real people—children, old people, teenagers, prisoners, parents who can't feed their children, refugees, victims of torture.

We cannot be friends with the poor and not have that vision. The vision begins when we tend "one of the least of these." We see in that one person Jesus. We ache for the pain of that one person. We struggle with a vision—which if acted upon—would alleviate that suffering.

We interpret that overarching vision so that others can see it too. The vision extends the boundaries of what is possible. The vision sweeps aside the conventional "truths" of those who trust in false gods. Drawn by its power and truth, others also see the vision. The spark ignites their energies.

Together, we find the way and begin to act. A vision will have a handle the size of my hand. And there will be a place for other hands. "A vision is a dream with clothes on," said Martin Luther King, Jr.

The Nightmare Ends Where Justice Begins

"Righteousness (justice) and peace will kiss each other" (Ps. 85:10, RSV). They have an intimate relationship. The slogan "If you want peace, work for justice," may sound trite, but it's true. When you work for justice, you will notice its intimate relationship to peace.

Two persons who talked about peace cried about it when they did. Jesus wept over Jerusalem saying, "How often would I have gathered you . . . would that . . . you knew the things that make for peace!"

Jeremiah, the weeping prophet, also knew the intimate relationship between justice and peace. "They have healed the wound of my people lightly, saying, 'Peace, Peace,' when there is no peace." True peace springs from just actions, not insincere words.

"Lord, when did we see you. . . ?" is a question that will not go away. Is a new confessing church forming, one committed to a vision of biblical justice and peace?

Visions of Converting Swords into Services

The architects of the Pentagon drew plans for a large five-sided building in Washington, D.C., to house the Department of Defense. They could not imagine, though, that it would be needed as a military headquarters following World War II. They had different visions for it after the war ended.

The Pentagon, built on a former swamp called "Hell's Bottom," is a mile around the outside. A city within itself, it provides office space for up to 30,000 people on its eighteen miles of corridors. The building occupies thirty-four acres, surrounded by sixty-seven acres of asphalt with parking space for 9,849 vehicles. An indoor shopping center hallway has enough room for cars to pass. About 60,000 meals are served daily in its 18 dining rooms. Built in sixteen short months, the building was completed in 1943 at an approximate cost of $83,000,000.

Inside the Pentagon, one is constantly reminded of the architects' dream. In its rings, corridors, and bays, staff people move on broad ramps. Why ramps? After World War II, this stronghold of the military would be converted into a great center for healing, so the ramps were designed for wheelchairs and stretchers! The Pentagon would be converted into a hospital—the biggest and best in the world.

The original plan to convert the Pentagon into a hospital was a crucial effort to redirect society. It would re-align national priorities. When an economy diverts from military to domestic production, it is called "economic conversion." The Bible calls it turning swords into plowshares. It has not happened—yet.

But dreamers dream on. They know the biblical truth. "Where there is no vision, the people perish." They continue to dream of swords converted into healing—even at Hell's Bottom.

CHAPTER 6

A New Confessing Church?

A new wind of Christian conscience is blowing across the church in North America. It is causing amazing changes.

Until recently, the structures of the Cold War and the arms race seemed unchangeable. However, the 1980s ended with stunning political changes in Eastern Europe. Our imaginations raced to catch up.

Much of the energy for change came from the peace witness of the East European churches. Churches have been examples of resistance, protectors of human dignity, and resources for political and social change. The power and endurance of religious communities in those lands is remarkable.

This quiet revolution in the churches is based on new ways of hearing, trusting, obeying. Few have understood the full force of this new wind. It is transforming parts of the Christian community. People who have lived nightmares are dreaming new visions.

Why the Winds Have Come

Much of the church in the U.S. was lulled by government assurance that use of terrible nuclear weapons was unthinkable. They were for deterrent or "threat" purposes only.

Then the church awoke to realize that first use of the weapons was not only contemplated, but lauded. The Canadian church came out of the closet when it realized its government was violating its own policy. The Canadian government had said no to nuclear weapons. But it then allowed nuclear weapons testing.

The new winds come from such sources as realization of the nuclear threat. Awareness of the link between military spending and hunger. A fresh look at Scripture, the God of creation, the Christ who calls.

Christians are asking questions about survival and faith. What does it mean to trust and obey God in a nuclear age? How can faith be real if it silently watches the nation build, deploy, aim, and threaten to unleash nuclear fire? Is not this the greatest heresy?

The winds are borne by a new understanding of the link between the higher standard of living in North America and the poorer standards elsewhere. We see the connection between military spending and hunger on the nightly news.

What the New Wind Is Doing

The new wind of the Spirit of God is blowing through North America—and around the world. Christians are no longer content to see injustice rule. Here are results of the fresh breath of God's spirit.

The wind is shattering habitual ways of thinking. The

old labels, left/right, are no longer useful. There is a new mix. The new "peace church" is beginning to look like the new community Jesus created.

The fresh wind is helping people to breathe. The stale air is being replaced by fresh air. The old argument about faith *or* action, trust *or* obedience, is really an argument about which is better, breathing in—or out.

Some of us argue that more study and prayer (breathing in) is the Christian thing to do. Some of us call for more action (breathing out). We will all, however, turn blue if we just breathe in *or* out. Either by itself causes a lack of the oxygen in the blood.

Improper breathing causes attitudes like "Who cares? One person can't make a difference. The poor will always be here. There will always be wars. Let's interpret peacemaking in a spiritual sense only."

Can you imagine Jesus separating trust from obedience? Must a sick world rush to death because Christians aren't breathing properly?

The wind is upending old modes of action. New understandings of Scripture are stirring fresh action. No longer is it business-as-usual. The old answers are not adequate. Stiff old wineskins have let precious wine drain away for too long. New wineskins can bulge and accommodate totally new and untried forms of action.

Not only do we see war rejected. We also see a new positive theology, a new program for peace. People who never dreamed they would be demonstrating at missile sites, going to jail, pleading with parliaments, visiting third-world countries, have done just that.

The winds are uncovering parts of the church's story. Some of these have been long ignored or simply unknown. Churches are looking again at their own history. Christian opposition to war has not gotten this much attention since the first centuries of the church.

During those first centuries—the ones closest to the New Testament—the church taught that going to war was contrary to Jesus' teachings. During the first 300 years, no Christian writer ever justified Christian participation in war. Then a dramatic change took place. Constantine became the first Christian to rule the Roman empire. Making Christianity the official religion, he used it for his own political ends. Within a hundred years, the empire required *all* soldiers to be Christian.

Christianity and militarism, poles apart since Christ, now joined to serve the state. Christianity lost its separate, prophetic nature. The early church's centuries-old faithfulness to pacifism came to a sudden end. Pacifism was no longer the main Christian response to war. It has never recovered from that change.

Today, however, the church is taking another look at peacemaking. The peace tradition of the early church has made a reentry onto the stage of both Christian thought and action. A new wind is blowing.

The new winds are separating the church's identity from the nations. We may be confused by Christ's seemingly contradictory commands. "Be separate [from the world]" (2 Cor. 6:17). "Go into all the world" (Matt. 28:19; Mark 16:15). Which way do we go? Both. The church draws itself apart from the world precisely so that it can be truly present in the world.

The new wind is helping the church to see itself called, like Abraham, to be a people in a "new land." Said God of God's new people,

"From the rocky peaks I see them,
   from the heights I view them.
I see a people who live apart.
   and do not consider themselves
      one [with] the nations" (Num. 23:9, emphasis added)

The church is separating itself from unquestioning allegiance to national and cultural traditions. The church and the nation are separate. In fact, the church is truly **present** to its nation only if **separate** from it.

The wind rearranges and integrates the church's priorities. It elevates peace and makes it a central part of its evangelism. Peace/justice are part of an inseparable message. Both are woven into one seamless garment. The wind brings new commitment no longer to tear the seamless garment.

No area of human endeavor escapes the wind. The new peace church wind supports the growing secular movements. It affects not only theology, but medicine, ecology, science, family life programs, and much more.

The new wind is reshaping the way the church thinks about its participation in war. We will discuss that in more detail in the next chapter.

How strong are the winds? Are the new Pentecost winds strong enough to totally change the church? Is the long hibernation of the Christian conscience now over? Or are the winds only a temporary gust of reaction? It is too soon to tell. My advice: keep watching the weather vane.

CHAPTER 7

A New Church Position on Warfare?

The new winds have refocused the questions. The old distinctions between pacifist and just-war adherents are breaking down and giving way to something new. Slavery—the kidnapping, buying, and selling of human beings—was once condoned. As concerned Christians once led a movement to abolish slavery, so today concerned Christians seek to abolish nuclear weapons.

Might we be seeing signs of a new Barmen confession arise from awakened consciences? Who would have thought that

• mainline church leaders would begin to wonder aloud whether they should declare themselves "peace churches."

• a well-known evangelist would declare, "I have confused the kingdom of God with the American way of life."

43

• the American bishops of the Roman Catholic Church would write a pastoral letter denouncing all nuclear arms?

• renowned bishops would call the church to resist government military policies?

• a top military leader would say to the National War College, "The greatest challenge to all that we do now comes from within the churches."

Three Ways to Look at War

Christians have looked at war in three basic ways: holy war, the just war, and Christian pacifism.

Holy war. Some people say the state's military policies are always legitimate and should always be followed. Such persons make no examination of the individual conscience, nor do they make independent judgments. Their obedience to authority is absolute and unquestioning. They make nonparticipation in war seem irresponsible and intolerable.

You will hear from them comments such as, "I leave peace and war policy issues to the experts who know best. It is not my place to complain or challenge the policies of the governing authorities. Our national interest is God's interest. God is always on our side. Patriotism for my country is the same as loyalty to God. Therefore, any means can be used to defend it.

"We have peace through strength, so peace comes through military power. Nuclear weapons are justified because they deter the other side through mutually assured destruction! War is fighting for God."

Just war. Just-war adherents believe that under certain circumstances participation in war may be the lesser of evils and therefore, "just." The just-war tradition seeks to limit violence by establishing rules by which war should be waged. War is justified, according to these measures, when its good outcome—the restoration of justice—outweighs the harm it will cause.

Just-war theory says that violence can be justified if a greater good or justice is accomplished. But the means of violence has to meet particular standards. For example, innocent people and noncombatants may not be killed.

Two just-war concepts bear special scrutiny, First, *discrimination.* Armed forces must discriminate between military and nonmilitary targets. They should seek to keep noncombatants and civilians out of danger.

Second, *proportionality.* The amount of armed force must be in reasonable proportion to the end that is to be achieved.

Christian pacifism. There are many kinds of pacifists. The historic peace church tradition bases its pacifist convictions on the New Testament. These pacifists believe that participation in war is *always* sin.

They say, "Participation in war is forbidden for the Christian. To take vengeance into our own hands is to assume a role which belongs to God. Christ calls us to love our enemies, not to destroy them. Christians are called to faithfulness, not to compromise. When Jesus told Peter to 'put up the sword,' he disarmed every Christian."

Many wrongly assume that "pacifism" is the same as "passivism." Some assume that the only alternative to going to war is *doing nothing*. That may be a definition of some kinds of pacifism—but not New Testament pacifism.

The term *pacifist* comes from the Latin word for "peacemaking." For the New Testament pacifist, the *no* to participation in war has its source in the *yes* of active peace building.

True pacifism is not unrealistic submission to an evil power. It is rather courageous confrontation of evil by the power of love. It demands nonviolent, non-military ways to resolve personal and international conflict.

New Testament pacifists are committed to nonviolent ways of resolving conflicts, even if that means personal suffering or death. The pacifist role is not easy. Pacifists are not *passivists*. Pacifists are busy. They assume risk and costly responsibility.

Common Ground

The gulf between the two most common Christian positions, just war and pacifism, has been deep. The old arguments produced nothing creative and useful. The arguments sounded something like this.

"Pacifists are to be commended, even admired, but they are irresponsible. We who know what the world is really like cannot share their naive optimism." That was the familiar observation in mainline Protestant and Catholic circles.

The reply of the historic peace churches was equally familiar. "The principles of just war may sound noble, but in practice they merely pronounce a blessing upon wars, nations, and ideologies."

Just-war adherents are not warmongers, and pacifists are not cowards. Both agree on the need for moral restraint on the use of violence. Both agree that there has never been a time so dangerous, so in need of the voice of Christian conscience. Both are hearing the voice of God in new ways as they struggle with the old questions.

The old distinctions between just-war and pacifist churches are breaking down. Both the just-war and the peace churches are moving toward a positive united peacemaking task. This shows in both trust and obedience, both theology and practice.

The renewal is based on prayer, preaching, commitment, and sacrifice. Suddenly these two groups find a common and mutually enriching ground between them. Never have they had to take each other so seriously. Never have they needed to listen to each other so carefully.

The historic peace churches and those of other traditions are far from having a unified peace position. They are moving toward it, however, not away from it.

An example of this is Christian Peacemaker Teams, a project sponsored by various peace churches, which takes a unique approach to peacemaking. These small, committed groups identify with suffering people. Their goal is to reduce violence through mediation of conflicts. They cultivate justice through the caring, peaceful, direct challenge of evil. Civil disobedience may be a small part of what is involved. But they say there are many loving ways to challenge evil in a loving, direct manner.

Temptations and Questions

The pacifist and just-war churches are now facing their own temptations. Each group is asking stimulating new questions of itself and of each other. Churches that hold to the *just-war position are asking these questions of themselves.*

1. Has our conscience been shaped by nationalistic thought more than by the voice of God?

2. Are we tempted to rely on "experts" in governments, rather than our own church teachings?

3. Because we have not taken the pacifist position, have we looked hard enough for nonviolent and nonmilitary solutions?

4. Have we just-war religious communities found it awkward, if not impossible, to support our own conscientious objectors? These youth reject the draft precisely *because* they followed our just-war teaching into selective conscientious objection.

5. Have we blessed actions that cannot be justified by the teachings of Jesus or even our own just-war criteria? Have we too easily declared wars just? Has our participation in wars been almost automatic and uncritical?

The pacifist churches are asking these questions of themselves.

1. Do we say, "Because I am not a participant in war I am not responsible for it"? Are we tempted to feel self-righteous and free from bearing our share of the national guilt? Are we tempted to wash our hands of fault and also responsibility?

2. When we state our "no" to participation in war, do we point out another way clearly enough?

3. Do we put ourselves at risk to stand between warring factions?

4. Do we state clearly and often that "in Christ's name I can not, will not consent to this violence?" Are we a living witness to the gospel of peace?

5. Are we vigorous enough in seeking ways to prevent the violence of injustice, starvation, disease, and murder? The seeds of nonviolence are sown by example or they are not sown at all. Are we hoping for a harvest where we have not sown?

Both just-war and pacifist church leaders agree there is much to confess. Both are calling on the religious community to these steps:

1. Make a stronger witness to political leaders about the immorality of weapons as a way to peace.

2. Pursue a better thought-out alternative to global security.

3. Support conscientious objectors of all kinds, including those who break the law in refusing to go to war or pay taxes for war. The church must offer them moral support, pastoral care, counseling, and financial support. The religious community must respect their conscience even if not in agreement.

4. Advocate that policymakers change the law, so all conscientious objectors have the rights now granted most easily to religious conscientious objectors.

5. Provide a more prophetic witness coupled with an intense pastoral ministry to those who work in the nuclear and other weapons industries.

6. Respect the call of conscience to apply just war and pacifist teachings to other citizen roles, including tax-paying.

7. Call Christians to invest themselves in more positive peacemaking.

8. Give significant place to teaching against war in the religious nurture of children and adults.

Both just-war advocates and pacifists are now asking these questions: If it is wrong to participate in war, and if it is wrong to sit back and do nothing, what are we doing to point to a new way? What are we doing to be divine leaven in the human dough? What are we doing to create a living society inside a dying one?

Churches Express the New Wind of the Spirit

Major church bodies, Catholic and Protestant, have spoken forcefully against the arms race. Many denominations have instituted substantial study-action programs on peacemaking. Notable among these are the Presbyterian Church USA, the United Methodist Church, the American Baptist Churches, and the Evangelical Lutheran Churches of America and the United Church of Christ which has just changed its identity from a just-war to a "just peace" church. Congregations and their conference bodies are becoming active peacemakers in creative new ways. The threat of nuclear war and economic violence are causing Christians around the world to study the Bible, pray, plan, and act to change their country's values.

Catholic Bishops. The Catholic bishops have issued a peace pastoral entitled *The Challenge to Peace: God's Promise and Our Response.* In it they carefully reexamined those areas in which the Roman Catholic Church has traditionally supported U.S. military policy. They asked questions that do not go away.

Do the exorbitant costs, the general climate of insecurity generated, the possibility of accidental detonation of highly destructive weapons, the danger of error and miscalculation that could provoke retaliation and war. . . .

Do such evils or others attendant upon and indirectly deriving from the arms race make the arms race itself a disproportionate response to aggressions?

How many deaths of noncombatants are "tolerable" as a result of indirect attacks—attacks directed against combat forces and military targets which nevertheless kill noncombatants at the same time?

The bishops answered the questions. They said,

Peace is God's gift and God's intention for all creation. We are called to respond to God by doing those things which not only inhibit war. Also we are called to create the political and social climate which will build peace on earth.

It is therefore not only wrong to *use* nuclear weapons. It is wrong to *threaten* to use them. It is wrong even to *possess* them.

We commit ourselves to noncooperation with our country's preparations for nuclear war. On all levels—research, development, testing, production, deployment, and actual use of nuclear weapons—we commit ourselves to resist in the name of Jesus Christ.
      —The Sojourners Community

Methodist Bishops. A recent plea by United Methodist bishops asked their members to become "defenders of God's good creation; and to pray without ceasing for peace in our time."

> We write in defense of Creation. We do so because the Creation itself is under attack. Air and water, trees and fruits and flowers, birds and fish and cattle, all children and youth, women and men live under the darkening shadows of a threatening nuclear winter.
>
> We call the United Methodist Church to more faithful witness and action in the face of this worsening nuclear crisis. It is a crisis that threatens to assault not only the whole human family but planet Earth itself, even while the arms race itself cruelly destroys millions of lives in conventional wars, repressive violence, and massive poverty.

Abolitionist Covenant

In 19th-century U.S., slavery was accepted even by the churches. Yet, thousands of Christians took a stand against it. They believed it wrong for any person to buy, sell, or own another. They began to understand that slavery was more than a political question. It was a question of faith.

These Christians preached that followers of Christ could have no part of the institution of slavery. Refusing to cooperate with it, they worked for its abolition. They were called "abolitionists." To abolish slavery seemed like an absurd, unattainable goal, but the abolitionists insisted that God required nothing less.

In the 20th century, thousands of believers have

come to see that weapons of destruction are more than a political question. They are a question of faith. Even though the goal seems unattainable, they are called by God to work for their abolition.

These people of faith have written a "New Abolitionist Covenant." It is based on prayer, preaching, commitment, and sacrifice. It says,

> Our response as Christians begins with repentance for almost four decades of accepting nuclear weapons. Repentance in a nuclear age means noncooperation with preparations for nuclear war and the turning of our lives toward peace. . . . The fruits of our repentance will be made visible in our active witness and leadership for peace.

The struggle for peace will be at least as arduous and costly as the battle against slavery, and probably more so. The testimony of the abolitionists remains the hopeful story of how a vision of faith became a reality.

Historic Peace Churches

Mennonites (descendants of the Anabaptists), the Church of the Brethren, and the Religious Society of Friends (Quakers) have taken positions against participation in war. Because they have done so, they are called the "historic peace churches." During their earliest centuries their preaching of nonviolence and their refusal to bear arms resulted in suffering, not only at the hands of the state, but even by other churches.

But their "no" to war has meant a "yes" to other peacemaking endeavors. Their peace testimony has taken many forms of expression. They have created and maintained extensive programs of relief, reconstruction, and reconciliation.

Far beyond what one would expect from their small size, they carry out significant efforts to assist the victims of natural catastrophes, war, and oppression. Their pioneering efforts in work camps, international exchanges, and extensive voluntary service programs have given concrete assistance across boundaries of race, nation, and class.

As one example, Mennonite Central Committee, a relief and service agency, has at any one time 1,000 young adults serving fifty-two countries. These volunteers are trained for work in health, education, and agriculture. The historic peace churches have a greater percentage of people who have experience working in other countries than any other church.

CHAPTER 8

Who Is My Neighbor?

Mary and Joseph were in our church on Christmas Eve. I am not referring to children dressed up as Mary and Joseph. This Mary and Joseph were real people. Like the biblical Mary and Joseph, they were refugees fleeing to save the life of a child as well as their own.

María and José (Spanish for Mary and Joseph) had just arrived from Central America. In the candlelight of the Christmas Eve service, their faces showed a combination of fatigue, bewilderment, and relief.

"Thank you, my friends. This is a safe house. I am glad to be among you," said Joseph.

"Now we have hope that our family will be together again. God has answered our prayers," added Mary.

As we celebrated the birth of Jesus together with María and José, the Word acquired new flesh. We saw more clearly the suffering into which Jesus was born and understood the kingdom he came to inaugurate.

But it was illegal (according to our government) for us to shelter Mary and Joseph.

We were one of a growing number of "sanctuary churches" in the U.S. María and José came because a covenant group in the congregation had arranged for them and others like them to find temporary haven.

A First and Second Violence

The countries of Latin America, neighbors to the south, suffer a double violence. The first violence is economic: a gaunt poverty which causes disease and death from malnutrition. This plight of the poor is worsened by large North American corporations. They reap huge profits from the low paid labor of the poor.

The second violence is military. Brutal dictatorships, instead of bringing reforms to help the poor, bring repression. And when the U.S. exports weapons and military training, the military violence increases.

Why were María and José fleeing? Some of the refugees who came to us bore on their bodies marks of torture. All bore in their minds the intimate knowledge and dread of it.

We North Americans listened to their shocking, soul-shaking stories. The tales of torture included "disappearances," midnight raids, beatings, bones deliberately broken, hanging by the wrists, acid burns, gang rapes, unborn babies torn from the womb, beheadings.

We heard about death squads. These squads, known to be connected to the military, have assassinated many. They are primarily responsible for the disappearance of thousands. Those who "disappear" are later found dead, with signs of torture. Indeed, violence claimed the lives of 60,000 Salvadoran civilians and 15,000 Nicaraguans in the 1980s.

What Is Their Crime?

The violence is directed at those who stand up for the most basic human rights. Generally, anyone who opposes the government, or is suspected of opposing it, is a likely target for the death squads. The only offense of those who flee is to try to better their own lives. Anyone who reaches out to help others is labeled "communist" and "subversive."

In special danger are persons who have participated in legitimate political and labor activities; those who try to achieve social progress; teachers and young men of military age. One refugee said,

> They pounded my hands with heavy metal rods, demanding responses to questions I couldn't answer. They asked for names, names. When I wouldn't answer they hit me in the chest over and over.

They had used electric shock, pulled out his fingernails, hung him by his wrists, burned him with acid, and broke his arm.

Some who flee for their lives are welcomed by the U.S. government. Too many others are misidentified as economic rather than political refugees. Thousands who come to this country and begin new lives are sought out and deported, contrary to U.S. laws and United Nations commitment. They are forcibly returned home, sometimes despite visible signs of torture or knowledge that their names appear on death lists. Some are killed immediately upon return. Others may live a month before their badly mutilated bodies are found.

North Americans became aware of the martyrdoms in Central America. They looked at their gate and saw Lazarus. He would be killed by pursuers if no one opened the gate. And when Lazarus had successfully crawled under the gate to relative safety in our yard, he was arrested and sent back sometimes to torture and death. These martyrdoms shocked North American Christians from their sleep. Their faith cried out for action.

Base Christian Communities

The south wind blowing across North America brought new currents of spirituality and church life from the Christians to the south. There "base Christian communities," centering on Bible study, holy communion, and prayer were forming. The life-threatening situations increased rather than hindered this growth. These communities began making their own Barmen-type declarations "in life and in death."

Many bishops and priests, formerly honored guests at the tables of the powerful and rich, have now become companions of the poor. Clergy who used to bless political prisoners before their executions now have become political prisoners themselves. Many have been killed or have disappeared.

Serious Bible study has always brought reformations. It did in the sixteenth century and still does. North American Christians too began to see Scripture through different eyes. With Central Americans, they rediscovered a God who leads people out of bondage.

They saw Jesus born into a family forced to become refugees. His birth had been announced to shepherds, not to the powerful. He ate with the common people. He opposed the hardships of economic poverty and military repression. He noted and decried injustices. He denounced the wealthy and the pious hypocrites.

Bad Systems Cause Injustice

Earlier, North American Christians had thought bad people created the trouble. They now learned that bad systems are implicated. They discovered that poverty is not accidental. They now knew poverty is a matter of structure, not only chance or poor personal choices. They had thought sin was something only private, inward, and personal. They now saw sin also as the alienation and division of whole societies.

Earlier they had thought Christians were called only to individual acts of feeding the hungry. They now saw that they are called to build structures and systems to feed the hungry. They now saw themselves as sitting at the head end of the world's table, eating too much. They saw that the ministry of Jesus was focused on the poor and the oppressed. He said,

> "The Spirit of the Lord is upon me, because he has anointed me to preach good news to the poor. He has sent me to proclaim release to the captives and recovering of sight to the blind, to set at liberty those who are oppressed. . ." (Luke 4:18, RSV).

Earlier, many North American Christians understood these words in the inward spiritual sense. Setting people free meant freedom from invisible chains.

They now saw that it also means physically opening the doors that imprison people and freeing them from economic and military violence. They saw that Jesus' spiritual concern extended to the physical, political, and social dimensions that imprison people.

These were questions that would not go away. Had their old interpretation muffled the clear sounds of the gospel? Had they spiritualized the Scriptures because the words made them feel uncomfortable?

North Americans Confront Suffering

As thousands of North Americans from all religious bodies traveled to Central America, they saw Lazarus for themselves. The visits changed their lives, their faith, and their obedience. Seeing faces is different from reading statistics. In each face they saw a Christian sister or brother, a cherished child of God.

They met Christians suffering from economic violence. They saw a poverty which middle-class North American Christians found hard to imagine. They heard of tortures they did not know the human mind could conceive.

These North American Christians returned to their home churches forever changed. Faraway villages with strange sounding names are now familiar places. The greatest symbol of the change is this: now when they pray for their sisters and brothers in Central America, they pray for them *by name*. Strong Christian ties now bind these Christians of the rich and poor Americas. The bonds are so deeply personal they can sometimes be expressed only with tears and prayers.

Churches Began to Act

North American churches began to draw the line and say, "In Christ's name we oppose this violence. We will take action, and we are prepared to take the consequence. We must obey God, not humans."

How could we turn our faces? This slaughter is wrong. "We can establish a clear moral principle," said one rabbi. "To save a human life is sufficient reason to break a law. If lives are at stake and the law stands in the way, the law must be sacrificed, not lives."

Serious Scripture study through new eyes told the church what to do about Lazarus at its gate.

> "When an alien lives with you in your land, do not mistreat him. The alien living with you must be treated as one of your native-born. Love him as yourself, for you were aliens in Egypt. I am the Lord your God" (Lev. 19:33-34).

> "I was a stranger and you invited me in. . . . Whatever you did it for one of the least of these brothers of mine, you did it for me" (Matt. 25:35, 40).

A sanctuary is a place of refuge, an island of safety in a sea of danger. It is no accident that our places of worship are called sanctuaries. In biblical times places of worship were offered as safe havens. People fleeing for their lives were safe only if they reached the sanctuary on time. No one could harm them there, not even the authorities. In the Old Testament era cities of refuge were established.

Those being pursued even for murder were to be received until things quieted down. "They will be places of refuge from the avenger, so that a person accused of murder may not die before he stands trial before the assembly. . . . The assembly must protect the one accused of murder from the avenger of blood" (Num. 35:12, 25).

First-century Christian communities also became places of refuge for slaves fleeing the cruel treatment of their masters. In the caves and catacombs of Rome, first-century Christians provided refuge, food, and shelter for each other. Here they hid from civil authorities. Their beliefs had made them "aliens in a foreign land."

The Church Opens Its Doors to Provide Sanctuary

Once again the church has opened its doors to provide support and protection to refugees of Central America. This sanctuary is an expression of the church's commitment to compassion, mercy, and the protection of human life.

Government officials are hesitant to enter church buildings and arrest refugees. Once inside the protection of a congregation, refugees are usually safe from deportation, even though they do not actually live in the church building.

In offering sanctuary, a church or synagogue declares its support and protection of refugees who lack legal documents. By this action, people of faith stand with those who have been made homeless.

A church does not declare sanctuary secretly. Sanctuary churches that invite the press to attend worship services thereby declare themselves a refuge for those pursued. At such open meetings the refugees typically cover their faces. They fear their families back home will be harmed if they should be identified.

The publicity gives Central Americans a platform for bearing public witness to their experience. The publicity informs other Americans about the desperate situation of the people of El Salvador and Guatemala.

Publicity also serves as an ironic kind of protection. Families that receive sanctuary and are well-known in their local communities are less likely to receive unfair treatment from the government or private individuals.

Over 50,000 Americans have followed their own consciences into the national sanctuary movement. There are now hundreds of sanctuary churches and synagogues "twinned" with congregations in Central America.

In addition, dozens of city governments have declared themselves sanctuary cities. Thousands of U.S. and Canadian cities adopt towns in Central America as "sister cities." There are twenty sanctuary universities and one sanctuary state. As Governor Tony Anaya declared New Mexico a "State of Sanctuary," he said, "The sanctuary movement is not fighting against unjust laws; it is fighting for the observance of just law."

National church agencies have published study materials on Central America. They have increased their mission presence there. Religious leaders visit Central America so they can speak with more authority. Other Christians have witnessed to government officials regarding what the churches in the region have observed. They not only embrace the refugee, but help the lawmakers to understand.

Here is a typical church statement.

> Therefore, we commend to American Baptist church-
> es the following: That we respect those churches that,
> responding to the leading of God's Spirit, are providing
> sanctuary for refugees fleeing certain suffering and
> death in Central America.
>
> (Resolution on Central America, June 1984)

The Churches Provide Services

Today, church people of many denominations offer
protection to the refugees from Central American
countries as they arrive in this country. This aid takes a
variety of forms.

The first objective is to shelter refugees from deportation and fear of death, especially those from El Salvador and Guatemala. This may mean secretly taking
them from place to place or helping them to reach
Canada, which has more readily accepted the refugees.

Second, churches provide a place to live, food,
clothing, medical services, and help in getting legal
counsel.

More than a century ago an "underground railroad"
was set up to help slaves sneak across the U.S. to freedom in Canada. Along the way people offered refuge
and help to find the next stop on the underground railroad. An underground railroad again transports refugees to Canada and freedom. Churches all over the
U.S. offer hospitality stops.

U.S. Government Response: Indictments, Trials, Convictions, Sentences

Government agents and informers have secretly visited worship services, Bible studies, and planning meetings of the sanctuary congregations. They have recorded such sessions with tape recorders concealed on their bodies. Sanctuary churches and centers have experienced numerous mysterious thefts of files and equipment, and destruction of their property. U.S. government prosecutors have admitted that they paid agents to go to church meetings, worship services, and Bible study groups to gather information.

Sanctuary workers suspect these actions are designed to frighten them so they will stop their actions. Sanctuary workers often hear themselves labeled communists. The Presbyterian and Lutheran churches sued the U.S. government to put an end to the illegal infiltration of churches and religious organizations.

Sanctuary workers have been charged with illegal offenses. Those so charged include Protestant ministers, Catholic priests, nuns, and other lay workers. A trial of sixteen sanctuary workers lasted seven months. Eight people were convicted for helping the refugees.

Some judges are sympathetic. But the courts often repeat the familiar, "You should not be involved in 'political actions.' Stick to your acts of 'charity' and prayer." Through Christian history the courts have been a place to speak to a truth that is different from conventional wisdom.

At her trial, Stacy Lynn Merkt spoke her questions that would not go away.

Recognizing that the people fleeing El Salvador and Guatemala are fleeing for their lives, realizing that the U.S. policy of sending rifles, bombs, planes, advisers, and training creates the refugees, we, the church as a body without borders, must take a stand.

We of the United States have the luxury of addressing these violences without dying. The costs for us are courtrooms . . . and prison time. I do not take either of those things lightly. The cost of doing nothing, sitting idly by is too high. If I examined Scripture in light of today's realities in Central America and the United States and do not act in some small way, I would not sleep at night.[8]

Questions for North Americans:

These winds from the South deposited new questions on our doorstep that will not blow away.

1. Does not the God of the Bible decry worship that is unconcerned about the plight of the stranger "outside the gate"?

2. Do we enter our sanctuaries with faces turned away from the human destruction outside?

3. Can we remain complacent with structures that benefit us even as they destroy others?

4. "Lord, when did we see you . . . a victim of torture? When did we see you a refugee turned away from our borders?"

CHAPTER 9

When Does Divine Obedience Require Civil Disobedience?

Daniel's three friends refused to go along with the crowd and bow down to the king's golden statue. At their trial they gave the reason for their civil disobedience. "Be it known to you, O king, that we will not serve your gods" (see Dan. 3:1-30, RSV).

The apostles were arrested and jailed for preaching a truth different from conventional wisdom. The early Christians were in the middle of everything . . . except the road. At their trial they declared, "We must obey God rather than humans."

Christians thrown to hungry lions in the Roman Colosseum said,

> "O ye Romans, all of you who have come to witness with your own eyes this combat; know ye, that this

punishment has not been laid upon me on account of
any misdeed or crime; for such I have in no wise committed."[9]

Anabaptists (from whom the historic peace
churches descended) took for granted that no Anabaptist can ever wield a sword. One Anabaptist expressed this deep belief.

> Naturally, he [the Christian] will be obedient to the au-
> thorities of this world as long as no conflict arises with
> his own conscience. Beyond that he is bound to deny
> such obedience since he is bound to a higher authority.
> Actually, he is already living in a world of a different di-
> mension, and therefore stands under its laws rather
> than under those of this world.

The Confessing Church said, in the Barmen Declaration, "The church of pardoned sinners in the midst
of a sinful world, with its faith and with its obedience . . . is solely God's property."

We are rich heirs of the bold, faithful, risky witness
of these ancestors in the faith. They found such creative ways to witness to the unique needs of their time.

These stories are powerful links in a chain of church
history that reaches from biblical times through the
Reformation and into the present. We add our own
links to the chain.

These stories are not antiques in a museum for us to
observe with curiosity and return to the shelf. In the
past few years, many Christians have joined this long
tradition of resistance of evil which sometimes expresses itself in civil disobedience.

Then, as now, the state tries people, who once in the dock, seem to put the state itself on trial.

Divine Obedience

Civil disobedience for the sake of divine obedience is not written in the margins of Christian history. It is written boldly across the center pages. It is at the very core of our biblical vision and tradition. We must never discount it as simply for the discontented and disgruntled. From the beginning of biblical history we find a revered form of holy disobedience. Think of how much of our Scripture was written from prison!

Why are God's sincere followers then and now so out of step with the majority? Jesus said those who did not follow him were "like children in the market place calling to one another, 'We piped to you, and you did not dance' " (Luke 7:32, RSV). Those who follow him are simply stepping to the tune of a different piper. They have decided to trust and obey the tune they hear.

Resistance to evil structures may be legal or illegal. Legal resistance includes political lobbying, voter power, economic boycott, peaceful political demonstrations.

Illegal resistance (civil disobedience) may include crossing lines, prayer vigils, peaceful demonstrations, military tax refusal, and even total noncooperation. It sometimes includes damage to property that is designed to kill (such as the symbolic "beating of swords into plowshares" with hammers on parts of nuclear weapons in production in factories).

Civil disobedience done for the sake of the kingdom

is truly divine obedience. It is a positive witness. It does not pull back and avoid. It reaches out. It embraces. The *no* of civil disobedience is deeply rooted in a profound *yes,* motivated by obedience to God's sovereignty. It is to "obey God rather than humans." It is also to accept responsibility for an evil that is ours. It is a way to pray, "Thy kingdom come, thy will be done."

What is Patriotism?

In court one war tax resister explained the answer to that question to the judge: "This may be a more profound patriotism than you are used to seeing—one that insists that real love of our country must be for the nation truly 'under God' and not the other way around. If we put our country first and our attempt to be faithful to God second, that will be 'contempt' of a far more serious nature."

Resistance Is Not Disrespect

Conscientious resistance, whether legal or illegal, is not driven by disrespect for government. It maintains a profound respect for the legitimate purpose for which government is established. Unquestioning obedience to the government is not the best citizenship to that government. Resistance does not mean a disengagement from government affairs. Rather it involves assuming responsibility at a different level. This civil disobedience is not defiance but obedience to a higher authority.

Actions that were once illegal have helped to end injustices. Slavery—the kidnapping, buying, and selling of human beings—used to be legalized by the gov-

ernment and sanctioned by the church. However, pe-
titions to government and acts of civil disobedience of
conscientious persons in the church ended its practice.

Conscientious objectors to military service are not
usually sent to prison as they once were. Women now
have the right to vote. Those who resisted earlier government orders suffered penalties, sometimes severe.
The possibility that they might fail in their attempt did
not deter them.

Christians generally have deep respect for law, and
rightly so. They understand law is designed for the or-
dering of society, for the common good. They do not,
therefore, take civil disobedience lightly, but only after great inner searching. The point comes when they
can no longer ignore the fact that human law sometimes violates divine law.

One demonstrator at a missile site said of her congregation, "We didn't want to deal with the issue, but
the issue was dealing with us."

Never have people of faith faced such demonic evil.
Of the 165 generations since Abraham, or 100 since
Jesus, none have faced the responsibility we do. The
sin of reliance on nuclear weapons is unique. By our
own hands we have created the awful means to end
human life as we now know it on this planet—to end
our covenant relationship with God.

To possess that power is to step over the boundary
and invade God's power. It is an attempt to grab the
steering wheel of history in our own hands. It is to
seize the crown. It is to play God.

The Legitimate Purpose of Government

According to biblical understanding, government was established to protect the innocent and to punish evil, to encourage the good and restrain harm, to serve peace and preserve the fabric of society.

Thomas Jefferson said, "The care of human life and happiness, and not their destruction, is the first and only legitimate object of good government."

The U.S. pledge of allegiance to the flag refers to "one nation under God." Christians must remember that it is the nation *under* God and not the other way around. They are called to *be subject* to the state. Sometimes they will obey the state. Sometimes, to be subject, they must disobey it and accept punishment.

Governments of course put "national interests" first—that is not surprising. But believers in God, the loving parent of the whole human family, dare not let nationalism be their highest allegiance.

Governments, even the best ones, can be wrong. No government is so bad that the Christian is to be no longer subject. No government is so good that the Christian need no longer think independently and accept suffering because of refusal to agree with its self-glorification and injustices.

It is the Christian's duty to encourage government to pursue its own claims with integrity, to work for justice, freedom, and human rights for all peoples. The church is not the master or servant of the state—but the conscience of the state.

These Questions Refuse to Go Away:

1. When the laws of the nation conflict with the laws

of God, what choices has the Christian?

2. How shall a Christian resist when world destruction is planned by government action?

3. Is the risk of inaction greater than the risk of wrong action?

CHAPTER 10

How Should We Speak Truth to Power?

Peace advocates and military officials live in two separate worlds. Peace advocates see military people as misguided, protected from reality by their offices. Military leaders see the peace movement as naive people meddling in a business they do not understand. Each group considers itself right and morally superior. Each usually preaches to its own true believers.

The dialogue between these parties is a crucial one. How can we keep it from being a dialogue of the deaf? If we consider military people as enemies to be beaten with our "truth," we will miss "an opportunity of giving them a chance to walk with us in a new direction" (Gandhi). We will miss learning valuable lessons.

Some would-be peacemakers show great concern for poor and oppressed people. But they seem to care little what happens to presidents, government officials, and others they dismiss as "no-good militarists."

Biblical truths spoken without love fall on deaf ears. We are to "speak the truth in love."

The Pain of Political Choices

During the painful days of the Vietnam war, a member of Congress expressed anguish. How could he reconcile his own political interests, the economic needs of people in his home district, and his moral standards? He was briefed on confidential material. It showed the extent to which the American people were being deceived about the conduct of the war.

Totally offended by the killing and angered by the deception, he yearned to express his outrage. He wanted to deliver a passionate speech on the floor of the House of Representatives. He never did. Why?

The district he represented contained several military facilities. He assumed the voters would turn him out of office if he took an antiwar stand. And, he dreamed of all the good he could do after the election if he remained silent now. The voters did not reelect him. Wrapped in regret, he said, "How much better if I had at least gone out of office for a cause!"

Soon after, he asked a question of a small group of us seeking meaningful ways to relate to legislators. His question still haunts me.

"Where were you when I needed you? You should have hung in with me. You should have urged me not to sell out! I might not have listened. But you should have urged me to live up to my own highest good."

As decision-makers are haunted by their silence, we too are haunted by ours. We share a duty.

Many factors enter into the formal decision-making

process of government. These social, economic, political, and military processes may be carried out in hearings, staff studies, committee sessions, and on the floors of congress and parliament. But deliberations on the moral and ethical aspects of these decisions take place deep within the legislators themselves. Sometimes they occur in loneliness, sometimes with a few trusted individuals in whom they confide.

Here is a tremendous opportunity. It may be difficult to believe, but North American citizens can become those respected and trusted few. It is not that hard, but it requires work and time to build the relationship. Some have already done this by correspondence and by visits with legislators. Some groups form small "delegations of conscience."

In such a role, we need not compete with Pentagon lobbyists who argue for weapons and their destructive power. We can draw on our expertise to speak to the moral and ethical dimensions of such decisions. Yet we must do so humbly recognizing the possible limitations of our vision.

We cannot remain silent. Whether in or out of Washington or Ottawa, we can observe and nurture every leaning toward disarmament, to reinforce every instinct toward nonviolent solutions to international conflict, to begin to expose every deception.

If we do not envision ourselves in such a role, are we willing to help name, appoint, and anoint others in our congressional district who would? Would we then support and encourage them in this critical task?

Whether or not decision-makers listen to us, we must speak the truth according to our own conscience.

CHAPTER 11

What Belongs to Caesar?

The decision to end the human race does not belong to Caesar. Therefore, tax dollars that wrestle that decision out of the hands of God do not either, say many.

Jesus Christ and Taxes

Taxes are the reason Jesus was born in Bethlehem and not at home. Caesar Augustus had asked for a "head count" and had put a new poll tax on the people. This personal tax began in the year A.D. 6.

The new tax was so resented that it caused a bloody revolt against Caesar. During this dangerous time Jesus said, "Render . . . to Caesar the things that are Caesar's, and to God the things that are God's" (Matt. 22:21; also Mark 12:17, Luke 20:25).

Because we quote this Scripture so much, it is important to look again at the historical setting.

This was Jesus' answer to a coalition of Pharisees and Herodians. We quote this Scripture so much. Let us look at its setting.

The Chief Priests had tried repeatedly to discredit Jesus. On one occasion they tried to "lay hands" on Jesus, but those priests feared the people. "So they watched him, and sent spies, who pretended to be sincere, that they might take hold of what he said, so as to deliver him up to the authority" (Luke 20:20, RSV).

A plan was devised. They would trap him with an unlikely combination of Pharisees and Herodians, two parties that had no love for each other. The Pharisees, upset by Jesus' teachings on the kingdom, had tried repeatedly to discredit him. This time they got together with the Herodians and planned to trap Jesus with a question.

The Pharisees had a principle against paying the tax. The Herodians, a party that favored King Herod, wanted to be on the good side of Rome, so they supported paying the tax. But these two factions had a common interest: getting rid of Jesus and his teachings. "Tell us . . . what you think. Is it lawful to pay taxes to Caesar, or not?" they asked.

They had set their trap well. If he said "Yes," he could be accused of giving support to the hated conquerors. If he said "No," he would be classified as an agitator. He then could be turned over to the Roman authorities for advocating rebellion. In hours or days he would be on death row.

Aware of their malice, Jesus first said, "Why put me to the test, you hypocrites?"

He then demanded, "Show me the coin used for

paying tax." They must have been embarrassed and uncomfortable, but what could they do but produce a coin? The coin they handed Jesus had Caesar's graven image on it.

"Whose likeness and inscription is this?" Jesus asked.

They said, "Caesar's."

The Coin

This coin was minted during the reign of Tiberius Caesar (A.D. 14-37). On it was Tiberius Caesar's own image, wearing the laurel wreath, the sign of divinity. This particular coin was a special form of the denarius and had been prescribed especially for taxpaying purposes.

The translated inscription read "Emperor Tiberius, worship worthy son of the worship worthy God." The other side of the coin read, *Pontif(ex) Maxim(us)* ("High Priest") and showed Caesar's mother sitting on the throne of the gods.

Now we are beginning to see why the story ends with the words, "And they were amazed!" The Pharisees insisted on exact adherence to religious law. They were good at condemning people for even the smallest violation of the law.

Yet look what they had in their pockets! It was blasphemy to suggest that Caesar was a god! That broke the first commandment. To carry any graven image broke the second commandment. The Pharisees taught that mere possession of the coin with its image of Caesar was sin! So when they showed Jesus the coin, they stood self-condemned. Attempting to embarrass

Jesus, they had exposed themselves.

The coin with Caesar's image belonged to the Caesar families. It had been minted especially for taxpaying purposes. The very fact that the Pharisees possessed the coin meant they paid the taxes they were asking Jesus about.

"Render . . . to Caesar the things that are Caesar's, and to God the things that are God's," said Jesus.

Jesus' answer seems to say, "As long as you have already sinned against your own law by using Caesar's money, go ahead and give Caesar what you have already decided belongs to him. You have already 'rendered unto Caesar.' "

Then without hesitation Jesus got to the core of his concern. "Render to God the things that are God's."

He had come through the designed test without appearing foolish and had instead left his questioners dumbfounded. "And they were amazed!"

When we ask the question about whether or not we should render military taxes to Caesar, we should be sure it is not a trick question.

Although there were many taxes in those days (temple taxes, land taxes, export taxes), the one in this story, the poll tax, was added by Caesar. Jesus was suggesting that because they had possessed the idolatrous coin, the real issue was no longer whether to pay taxes to Caesar. The real issue was faithfulness to God.[10]

Our loyalty to Caesar is secondary to our loyalty to God. Governments derive their authority from a higher power. While a government may claim absolute authority, its laws cannot override God's higher laws.

Both the Herodians and the Pharisees must have

suspected Jesus would oppose the tax. Otherwise their question would not have been a trap. In any case, Jesus was accused of refusing to pay the tax, of not rendering to Caesar. His opponents did not give up. "The whole assembly rose and led him off to Pilate. And they began to accuse him, saying, 'We have found this man subverting our nation. *He opposes the payment of taxes to Caesar* and claims to be Christ, a king' " (Luke 23:1-2, emphasis added).

The crucifixion followed. Later, when many Christians refused both military service and taxes for Caesar's wars, they died as martyrs.

In Whom Do We Trust?

The question of what belongs to God and what belongs to Caesar will not go away. To deal with it we are forced to deal with other questions. In whom do we trust? Who is our neighbor?

"In God We Trust" is engraved or printed on all U.S. currency. When we pay taxes, over half of these "In God We Trusts" go to fund the U.S. military. We are told to trust the "nuclear umbrella" and the institutions charged with using it.

Despite the slogan on our currency, we are increasingly called to put our trust in weapons of mass destruction, gods of metal. And this in the face of the deaths of 40,000 children daily from lack of an adequate diet and inexpensive vaccines.

The weapons have been named for "devil gods"— Trident, Titan, Poseidon. Are we sacrificing the children to the gods? Like gods, these weapons are helpless to save us. They do not have any sensitivity to their potential victims. Of these the Scripture says:

> Their idols are silver and gold,
>   made by the hands of men.
> They have mouths but cannot speak,
>   eyes but they cannot see;
> they have ears, but cannot hear,
>   noses, but they cannot smell;
> they have hands but cannot feel,
>   feet, but they cannot walk;
>   nor can they utter a sound with their throats.
> *Those who make them will be like them,*
> *and so will who trust in them.*
> —Psalm 115:4-8 (emphasis added)

The great commandment to love God calls us to revere the source of all life and to refuse to pay tribute to idols.

Christians do not reject weapons because they are too dangerous, but because they are too weak. Weapons are too weak to save us. They are too weak to turn enemies into friends. They are too weak to minister, to feed, clothe, and house the suffering Christ in disguise.

Each side in warfare "trusts God." In World War II, U.S. In-God-We-Trusts were buying weapons to kill German soldiers. Each German soldier wore a belt buckle which read, "God with us."

Constantine's "Christian" armies fought under the sign of the cross. In the name of Christ the crusaders slaughtered. Inquisitors tortured "heretics."

Our money is a trust *from* God.

Trust in God is not merely a mental exercise. Do we

let our insecurity turn us to *trust* in the bomb rather than in God-given principles of justice, freedom, and faith?

Who Is My Neighbor?

We know who our neighbor is. When Jesus dealt with this question, he told us how to *live as neighbors.*

Christians in developed countries today pay more in taxes for the support of the military than they give to the church and all other benevolent causes. With one hand Christians give generously for life-building purposes that ease human suffering. With the other hand, they pay military taxes that can cancel the good they have done. We pay to relieve suffering and we pay to increase it. We pray for peace and pay for war. How taxes relate to war and peace becomes morally crucial for more and more people.

Power of Conscience

Conscience is not mere opinion. It is a force which dictates how we are to live. We are aware we have a conscience when we follow it and pay a personal cost as a result, or when we do not follow it and experience some pain. It will not let us go. One of my favorite definitions comes from Pope John XXIII.

> In the depths of his conscience, man detects a law which he does not impose upon himself, but which holds him to obedience. Always summoning him to love good and avoid evil, the voice of conscience can when necessary speak to his heart more specifically: do this, shun that.

A statement of true belief, of conscience, has a compelling power. It causes others to examine their own conscience. Someone said, "There is nothing more powerful than the individual acting out of conscience." This brings the collective conscience (or conscience of a whole people) to life.

Will Power, "Can't" Power

Hundreds of conscientious objectors suffered, a few even died, in prison for their beliefs during World War I. Partly as a result, legal provision was made for conscientious objectors shortly before World War II. At that time, someone reportedly commented to the general at the head of the Selective Service, "You certainly have to admire the peace churches for their will power."

The general replied, "I don't know about their will power, but they certainly have a lot of 'won't' power."

But conscientious objection is not defined by won't power. It is not that conscientious objectors *won't* participate in military service or payment. They *can't* because conscience forbids it. When we explain the difference between *won't* and *can't* we have gone a long way toward defining conscience.

Conscientious objectors say that it is the *ultimate right* of the conscience not to participate in the killing of another human being—whether that participation be physical or financial.

Conscientious War Tax Resistance

Those who cannot pay and therefore resist the military portion of their taxes are usually called war tax resisters. "We are war tax resisters," says John Stoner, "because we have discovered some doubt as to what belongs to Caesar and what belongs to God, and have decided to give the benefit of the doubt to God."

Stoner adds, "In a day when the authority of the church is disobeyed everywhere with impunity, it is . . . a shock to observe the fanaticism with which Christians insist that Caesar must be given every cent he wants."

War tax resistance was not invented in the twentieth century. It is an ancient dilemma. From the earliest Christian times to the present, Christians have struggled over this dilemma. Here is a part of a confession written by a sixteenth-century martyr.

> Therefore we are gladly and willingly subject to the government for the Lord's sake, and in all just matters we will in no way oppose it. When, however, the government requires of us what is contrary to our faith and conscience—as swearing oaths and paying hangman's dues or taxes for war—then we do not obey its command. This we do not out of obstinacy or pride, but only out of pure fear of God. For it is our duty to obey God rather than man. (1560 Hutterite Claus Felbinger, confirmed this perspective in a written confession.)

Legal Losses, Moral Witness

Conscientious objectors continue to be tried in court. The courts consistently deny the claim that religious freedom is violated when people are forced by law to pay for killing against the dictates of their conscience.

Legal losses, however, do not prevent a forceful

moral witness. The courts often become new pulpits for a witness that rouses consciences which have yielded to majority opinion.

A Variety of Tax Responses

Conscientious war tax resistance expresses itself in many ways. Each person or couple must decide the appropriate way to respond to conscience.

Some enclose a letter of protest with their tax form to explain their revulsion for killing. Others choose to withhold a token symbolic amount and explain why. Some withhold the amount (approximately thirty-five percent) with is for *current* military spending. Some like Archbishop Hunthausen withhold roughly fifty percent in opposition to military spending. Some refuse only the amount going to build nuclear weapons. Some refuse to pay any taxes.

War tax resisters do not keep the resisted tax money for themselves. They use it for relieving human needs, or they hold it in escrow until the government can assure them that the money will not be spent killing people.

Many change their lifestyle and employment, even to the point of living below the taxable income level.

Working Toward a Legal Alternative

Over half of every U.S. income tax dollar is spent for current and past military purposes.[11] Taxpayers who are conscientiously opposed to such participation must either violate their beliefs or the law. Both Canadian and the U.S. law recognize the right of conscientious objection to military service and allow them to do alternate service instead.

But no such recognition exists for conscientious objectors to the use of their taxes for killing. Some are asking for such recognition in law. They are asking for alternative service for drafted dollars.

If these new laws are passed, here is how they would work. Conscientious objectors (like everyone else) would pay 100 percent of their taxes. But the military portion would go into a separate fund called the (Canadian or U.S.) Peace Tax Fund.[12]

Money in the Peace Tax Fund would be used for nonmilitary purposes—for research into nonviolent and nonmilitary ways to resolve international conflicts, and for disarmament efforts.

Some would turn swords into plowshares, an economic conversion. For example, if a factory stopped making bombs and started producing medical supplies, all the factory workers would have to be retrained. The whole factory would have to be re-tooled. This is expensive. Where would the money come from? Money in the Peace Tax Fund could be used.

Similar peace tax initiatives exist in a number of countries. The dilemma of taxes for war has existed in many centuries, in many countries. Sixteen countries attend the biyearly conferences of War Tax Resisters and Peace Tax Campaigns.

Regarding Peace Tax legislation in the U.S. Congress, we find a deficient understanding of conscience. We must therefore struggle to clarify its uncompromising claim on our lives.

One person wrote with clarity to members of Congress.

> For me to pay the military portion of my taxes is a sin on at least four counts.
>
> One is the sin of suicide against my own person (in the event of nuclear war). Second is the sin of premeditated murder. Third is the sin of injustice against two-thirds of the world's people, who are hungry, sick, and ragged through no fault of their own. Fourth is the sin of idolatry, for trusting in armaments rather than in God. I am my country's good servant, but God's servant first.

We have made a good beginning, but many more people will have to interpret their conscientious inability to pay to kill another, both in their words and actions.

Meanwhile, however, there is more ferment "back home." A growing number of people find themselves unable to pay military taxes in defiance of their consciences. Church bodies are speaking out. As military spending soars, conscience is harder to set aside.

Employer Resistance to Collecting War Taxes

The struggle of what belongs to Caesar and what belongs to God was, until lately, assumed mostly by the individual—the individual and God; the individual and conscience; the individual and the state (revenue collectors, the courts).

Because many thoughtful persons have become conscientious war tax resisters, religious communities cannot avoid examining their own involvement. Church bodies are now involved on two levels. Most affirm conscientious war tax resistance as an authentic Christian witness.

Many also offer financial support through "conscience support funds"[13] which provide money to help pay interest and penalties. Churches also provide moral support through prayers and active support by accompanying individuals at court hearings, at meetings with revenue collection agents, or at auctions and seizure of personal property.

Second, employers face their own involvement in payment for war through the system of employer tax withholding (pay as you earn). During World War II, a new tax system was devised to accommodate growing military expenses. Since then each employer is required by law to withhold a percentage from the employee's paycheck and forward it to the government.

The tax withholding system has to a large extent made every taxpayer a supporter of the war effort even before he or she receives the paycheck. Therefore, some employees are asking their church employers not to violate their consciences. These individuals are asking their employers not to withhold and send to the government the military portion of the federal tax from their paycheck.

This places the burden of conscience squarely on the employers who must respond to conscientious objectors on their staffs. Because employers are directly and involuntarily involved in the withholding system, many religious employers are caught in a difficult place. They stand between the conscientiously held beliefs of their faith tradition and the requirements of the tax system.

How can they teach their people to follow conscience—no matter what the cost—and then violate that conscience by giving to Caesar what the employee believes belongs to God?

Questions Church Bodies Cannot Avoid

Is it hypocritical to speak out against war while continuing to pay for it through taxes withheld and forwarded to the government?

What is a church employer's responsibility toward acts of conscience on the part of employees?

When should a church body be willing to pay a penalty for the cost of witness or the witness of an employee? Is it consistent with peace teachings to collect taxes that will be used for military purposes, regardless of the position of individual employees? The question is not about the size of the penalty, but what we perceive to be obedience to God.

If you thought that the decision-making process for the individual was difficult, consider the process for the corporate body! We all know that church bodies do not make decisions hastily. They set up committees. They hold workshops. They issue study guides. They wait for responses from their constituents. Then maybe after four or five years the question is ready for final debate and decision.

One never makes such a decision without looking the penalties straight in the eye. In this case, one gets an eyeful. Penalties for corporate bodies disobeying the tax laws are large.

A small but growing number of church bodies have decided to "obey God rather than humans." They can no longer in conscience continue to withhold tax dollars designed for killing. One body that made such a decision said, "Words are seldom heard but acts incarnating those words might be heard. As Christians, we must act. We are convinced that the foolishness of faithful acts may be wiser than all the wisdom of the world."[14]

See the appendix for further thoughts and guidelines on ways we can act to promote peace and justice.

EPILOGUE

Our Covenant Drama with God

In the drama of God's creation and redemption, our task is like improvisational theater. Improvisational theater is make-it-up-as-you-go drama. It does not have a script. The actor has no lines to memorize. No director details each gesture, expression, inflection. The unfolding drama relies entirely on an actor's ability to create the role as it is performed.

Special improvisational theater companies trais especially for this unique form of drama. It is a collective creation and takes a special skill. These players are told only how the play begins and ends. They are then given a plot which defines the action. The unrehearsed drama is created through the interaction of the players within the plot.

Each of us plays a part of the drama of God's covenant with humanity. No one remains off-stage. We are not mere robots in the hands of a director who gives us lines to memorize and actions to imitate. Without a script we are free to act creatively.

The beginning and end of our drama are not up to us. We had no part to play in Act I. God's creation furnished that. We have no part to play in Act III. To know the future "times and seasons" is for God alone. Our time on the stage comes in Act II. There our drama with God is played out. We are not to play God. We are not to play Act II as if it were Act III. If our company of actors forgets where it began and loses sight of its goal, the play will end in chaos and disaster.

Like all drama, our drama with God is full of conflict which seeks resolution. Sometimes it is structural, sometimes personal, but always the conflict exists.

In this kind of drama, peacemakers are free to play a variety of roles. Each actor must negotiate with other players, and define his or her role. Who am I in this story? To play my part well, I need to know *our* goal—what are we striving for? How will we reach our goal? With what forces do we strive?

As each member of the cast gets into character for a role in Act II, each must develop intricate skills. Each must fully know the covenant intent of the author of Acts I and III. Each must listen to God and each other.

The kingdom's creative power operates among players who know where they came from and are going. We listen to God's still, small voice. We listen to each other. We listen to those sisters and brothers not present with us—but whose sufferings and triumphs we have come to know.

Our peacemaking work and witness is our creative participation with God in fulfilling the covenant.

Appendix

***Tests, Cautions, and Benefits of Civil
Disobedience/Divine Obedience. Is it. . . .***

1. *Hearing God?* Divine obedience comes from deep listening to God at the center of the soul.

2. *Conscience Based?* The action must be rooted in conscience and not mere self-interest.

3. *Prayerful?* It must continue our prayer: "Thy kingdom come on earth as it is in heaven. Thy will be done."

4. *Community centered?* In addition to an individual inward journey, our truth must also be tested with the believing community. Not all need agree. But individual confession must be expressed.

5. *Nonviolent?* The means of expression must be nonviolent. No action taken in Christ's name harms another.

6. *Truthful?* This action comes from a commitment

to truth as best we know it and stands in sharp contrast to "conventional wisdom."

7. *Open?* The disobedience must be open, not hidden. It must be subject to public examination.

8. *Relating to victims?* It must state the Church's call to minister to victims. Action is always taken on behalf of current and potential victims of government policy.

9. *Non partisan?* Civil disobedience makes no distinctions between nationalities, religions, or political leanings. It speaks for *all* victims.

10. *Non-exploitive?* It does not use victims to make some political point. It does not select victims because of their "political usefulness."

11. *Against new bureaucracy?* The intent of civil disobedience/divine obedience is the return of governmental functions to those who are legally responsible for them. It establishes no new bureaucracy.

12. *Accepting of penalties?* The action must be taken with awareness of and willingness to accept the penalties.

13. *Opening dialogue?* The goal must be to communicate God's truth on behalf of the world's suffering.

14. *High regard for individuals?* Civil disobedience for the sake of divine obedience must address government leaders not just as officials, but as present and/or potential friends and followers of Christ.

15. *Making new friends, not new enemies?* The act of conscience may be done against the evil policies of the government. It is not an act against "evil individuals." Government officials are not the enemy. The most enduring thing we can achieve through such acts is new and loving relationships.

Cautions

Those who have disobeyed the state to obey God warn of these dangers.

1. *New enmity.* There is a temptation to turn an act of resistance into a confrontation between "us" and "them."

2. *Waging our kind of "war."* Even in nonviolent resistance, unless we accept deeply the spirit of nonviolence, we end up waging our own form of war. We become agitators rather than peacemakers if pride, anger, or cynicism creep in. We then only mimic the game of blame played out by warring nations.

3. *Feeling superior.* Words and acts of resistance must not be done from an exalted, superior position. Only those without sin may cast stones.

4. *Blame and hypocrisy:* Evil is not something external. It is hypocrisy to protest against something unless we admit that we also are responsible. Our action is not a "technique." It is a loving witness to God.

5. *Nonrepentant attitude.* To confront the destructive nuclear state is to face the worst current evil of humankind. But this confrontation is not a bout between evil and total innocence. We must repent of our share of the national guilt.

6. *Seeing evil as only external.* The evil that causes human suffering is an evil whose source is also within ourselves. The truth we preach has two edges. It must also penetrate the "preacher."

7. *Believing we have all truth.* We have something to teach, but we also have something to learn.

8. *Using the actions to solve our own problems.* Civil disobedience, like war, can be used to mask an inter-

nal emptiness. Such resistance, like the state itself, asserts power to hide a void.

9. *Trying to change others from the outside*. Because the evil we resist is so great, we are tempted to overlook the fact that we do not transform others from the outside. Their change will be internal, as ours must be. In the deep touching of each other's spirits we find mutual healing. Together we find a door through which to more fully enter the kingdom of God.

Benefits of Faith Based Resistance

1. *A new vision of another way*. Civil disobedience/ divine obedience points out injustice to victims and shows another way. Many will see and respond to the deeper Christian motivation.

2. *Witness which radiates new life and energy*. The witness of imagination and courage radiates outward and sparks new life and energy.

3. *Launching the church on an adventure of faith*. Divine obedience launches the church on an adventure of faith, uprooting it from the security offered by the surrounding culture, and leading it further into the security offered by God's kingdom.

4. *Changing minds, awakening conscience, softening hearts*. Strong actions which are taken at risk prick consciences and unveil the evils that people have ignored.

5. *New birth and new growth*. Resistance rooted in faith has a life-changing impact on churches and Christians. Those involved have their conversion deepened. Others, drawn by new vision, enter the kingdom of God. It affects their whole life.

6. *Gaining personal faith and responsibility*. Because success is not assured, one must deal with deeper issues of personal faith and personal responsibility.

7. *Experiencing the greatest change in ourselves*. The individual conscience will be the source of most of the change that occurs. Most of this change will, as with most acts of Christian obedience, happen in ourselves.

8. *Becoming willing to suffer*. Penalties of law, suffered in the interests of a moral cause, are honorable. They give validity to words of witness. Serving time in jail has become "a new monastery" for many.

9. *Restoring government policy to morally legitimate purposes*. As a resurrection people, Christians believe the course of history can be changed. Thus they try to restore government to its morally legitimate purposes.

10. *Renewal*. This outward step will direct us to our inward journey. The action may expose an emptiness at the center of our own lives. Inward renewal and growth can then inform the next action.

11. *We are not alone*. The miracle is not up to us. We are to bring the loaves and fishes out of which the miracle is made—to be sure the loaves are whole grain and that the fish are fresh.

Notes

1. Arthur C. Cochran, *The Church's Confession Under Hitler* (Philadelphia: Westminster Press, 1962).

2. Carl Sagan, *To Preserve a World Graced by Life*.

3. Center for Defense Information, Washington, D.C, *The Defense Monitor*, Vol. XVIII, No. 4, 1989.

4. George Zabelka (a retired diocesan priest in Lansing, Mich.), in Jim Wallis, ed., *Peacemakers: Christian Voices from the Abolitionist Movement* (San Francisco: Harper & Row) pp. 14-20.

5. 40,000 children die daily of hunger and other preventable causes. U.S. Committee for UNICEF, 331 East 38th Street, New York City, NY, 10061. (212 686-5522.)

6. $29,000 every hour since the birth of Christ. Actual budget outlays for 1989 were $309 billion for current military spending, plus another $171 billion for past military (debts of wars, veterans benefits, etc.). The figure is $17,000 per hour if we use only "current military" spending.

7. Ruth Legar Sivard, *World Military and Social Expenditure, 1987-88*, 12th ed. (Washington, D.C.: World Priorities, 1987).

8. Stacy Lynn Merkt, Arthur Laflin, and Anne Montgomery, eds. *Swords into Plowshares* (Cambridge: Harper and Row, 1987), p. 137.

9. Ignatius, 111 A.D.; Thielemann, J. van Braght, ed., *Martyrs Mirror: The Story of Fifteen Centuries of Christian Martyrdom from the Time of Christ to A.D. 1660*, Fifth English Edition (Scottdale, Pa: Herald Press, 1950), p. 107.

10. Willard M. Swartley, from "The Christian and the Payment of Taxes

for War," a paper presented to the New Call to Peacemaking Conference at Green Lake, Wis., 1980.

11. Actual budget outlays for 1990 were: Current: 31.2%, past: 18.9%, total military: 50.1%, all other: 49.1%. Friends Committee on National Legislation, 245 Second Street, N.E., Washington, DC 20002. 4/90.

12. For more information, contact National Campaign for a Peace Tax Fund, 2121 Decatur Place NW, Washington D.C. 20008, phone 202 483-3751; or Conscience Canada, P.O. Box 601, Station E, Victoria, B.C. U8W-2P3, Canada, phone 604 384-5523.

13. For more information on one such project, contact War Tax Resisters Penalty Fund [a project of the Fellowship of Reconciliation], P.O. Box 25, North Manchester, IN 46962.

14. "A Resolution on Faithful Action Toward Tax Withholding," a report on the efforts to obtain CO status for the General Conference from requirements to withhold taxes from the wages of its employees, Minneapolis, Mid-Triennium Conference (1989).

For Further Reading

Eller, Vernard. *War and Peace from Genesis to Revelation*. Scottdale, Pa.: Herald Press, 1981.

Friesen, Delores, *Living More with Less: Study/Action Guide*. Scottdale: Herald Press, 1981.

Ginnis, Jim and Kathy. *Parenting for Peace and Justice*. Maryknoll: Orbis Books, 1982.

Janzen, Bernd, ed. *Communities of Conscience: Collected Statements on Conscience and Taxes for Military Preparation*. Washington, D.C.: Peace Tax Foundation, 1989.

Ruth-Heffelbower, Duane. *The Anabaptists Are Back: Making Peace in a Dangerous World*. Scottdale: Herald Press, 1991.

Sider, Ronald J. *Christ and Violence*. Scottdale: Herald Press, 1981.

Simon, Arthur. *Harvesting Peace: The Arms Race and Human Need*, Kansas City: Sheed and Ward, 1990.

Wallis, Jim, ed. *Peacemakers*. New York: Harper and Row, 1983.

Wallis, Jim, ed. *The Rise of Christian Conscience*. San Francisco: Harper and Row, 1987.

Yoder, John Howard. *What Would You Do?* Scottdale: Herald Press, 1983.

The Author

Marian Claassen Franz is executive director of the National Campaign for a Peace Tax Fund and also the Peace Tax Foundation. In pursuit of Peace Tax legislation, she interprets, to Congress, the conscience-driven values of persons who assert their right not to participate in killing other human beings through their military taxes.

Her pilgrimage, which began in rural Kansas, took her to Bethel College and Mennonite Biblical Seminary in Chicago where she graduated with master of religious education degree.

Over a decade of experience at Woodlawn Mennonite Church on Chicago's south side formed her values and direction. In a neighborhood of 2,000 people per square block—most African-Americans—many were caught in a cycle of poverty. She was distressed and grieved by the needless deaths—from poor housing conditions—of children of personal friends: death by rat bites, faulty wiring, lead paint poisoning, and fires. It is the Christian's duty, she maintains, not only to heal these wounds at a personal level, but to address the flawed government policies which contribute to suffering. In Washington D.C., prior to her present position, she was the director of *Dunamis*, an organization which embodies both the pastoral and prophetic dimensions of the church's witness to those in political power.

Marian has attended a number of international conferences of Peace Tax Campaigns and has been invited to speak and lead workshops in several European countries as well as in North America.

She and her husband, Delton, have three children, Gregory, Gayle, and Coretta. They are members of the Hyattsville Mennonite Church near Washington, D.C.

PEACE AND JUSTICE SERIES

This series of books sets forth briefly and simply some important emphases of the Bible regarding war and peace and how to deal with conflict and injustice. The authors write from within the Anabaptist tradition. This includes viewing the Scriptures as a whole as the believing community discerns God's Word through the guidance of the Spirit.

Some of the titles reflect biblical, theological, or historical content. Other titles in the series show how these principles and insights are practical in daily life.

The books in this series are published in North America by:

Herald Press
616 Walnut Avenue
Scottdale, PA 15683
USA

Herald Press
490 Dutton Drive
Waterloo, ON N2L 6H7
CANADA

For overseas distribution or permission to translate, write to the Scottdale address listed.